W.D. GANN INTERVIEW
by Richard D. Wyckoff

*The Law of Vibration Governs Stocks, Forex
and Commodities Movements*

William D. Gann

An Operator Whose Science and Ability Place Him in the Front Rank.

Sometime ago the attention of this magazine was attracted by certain long pull Stock Market predictions which were being made by William D. Gann. In a large number of cases Mr. Gann gave us, in advance, the exact points at which certain stocks and commodities would sell, together with prices close to the then prevailing figures which would not be touched.

For instance, when the New York Central was 131 he predicted that it would sell at 145 before 129. So repeatedly did his figures prove to be accurate, and so different did his work appear from that of any expert whose methods we had examined, that we set about to investigate Mr. Gann and his way of figuring out these predictions, as well as the particular use which he was making of them in the market.

The results of this investigation are remarkable in many ways.

It appears to be a fact that Mr. W. D. Gann has developed an entirely new idea as to the principles governing stock market movements. He bases his operations upon certain natural laws which, though existing since the world began, have only in recent years been subjected to the will of man and added to the list of so-called modern discoveries. We have asked Mr. Gann for an outline of his work, and have secured some remarkable evidence as to the results obtained there from.

We submit this in full recognition of the fact that in Wall Street a man with a new idea, an idea which violates the traditions and encourages a scientific view of the Proposition, is not usually welcomed by the majority, for the reason that he stimulates thought and research. These activities the said majority abhors.

W. D. Gann's description of his experience and methods is given herewith. It should be read with recognition of the established fact that Mr. Gann's predictions have proved correct in a large majority of instances...
-Mr. Gann:

"For the past ten years I have devoted my entire time and attention to the speculative markets. Like many others, I lost thousands of dollars and experienced the usual ups and downs incidental to the novice who enters the market without preparatory knowledge of the subject."

"I soon began to realize that all successful men, whether Lawyers,

12

Doctors or Scientists, devoted years of time to the study and investigation of their particular pursuit or profession before attempting to make any money out of it."

"Being in the Brokerage business myself and handling large accounts, I had opportunities seldom afforded the ordinary man for studying the cause of success and failure in the speculations of others. I found that over ninety percent of the traders who go into the market without knowledge or study usually lose in the end."

"I soon began to note the periodical recurrence of the rise and fall in stocks and commodities. This led me to conclude that natural law was the basis of market movements. I then decided to devote ten years of my life to the study of natural law as applicable to the speculative markets and to devote my best energies toward making speculation a profitable profession. After exhaustive researches and investigations of the known sciences, I discovered that the law of vibration enabled me to accurately determine the exact points at which stocks or commodities should rise and fall within a given time."

The working out of this law determines the cause and predicts the effect long before the street is aware of either. Most speculators can testify to the fact that it is looking at the effect and ignoring the cause that has produced their losses.

"It is impossible here to give an adequate idea of the law of vibrations as I apply it to the markets. However, the layman may be able to grasp some of the principles when I state that the law of vibration is the fundamental law upon which wireless telegraphy, wireless telephone and phonographs are based.

Without the existence of this law the above inventions would have been impossible."

"In order to test the efficiency of my idea I have not only put in years of labor in the regular way, but I spent nine months working night and day in the Astor Library in New York and in the British Museum of London, going over the records of stock transactions as far back as 1820. I have incidentally examined the manipulations of Jay Gould, Daniel Drew, Commodore Vanderbilt & all other important manipulators from that time to the present day. I have examined

16

every quotation of Union Pacific prior to & from the time of E. H. Harriman. Mr. Harriman's was the most masterly. The figures show that, whether unconsciously or not, Mr. Harriman worked strictly in accordance with natural law."

"In going over the history of markets and the great mass of related statistics, it soon becomes apparent that certain laws govern the changes and variations in the value of stocks, and that there exists a periodic or cyclic law which is at the back of all these movements.

Observation has shown that there are regular periods of intense activity on the Exchange followed by periods of inactivity."

Mr. Henry Hall in his book devoted much space to "Cycles of Prosperity and Depression," which he found recurring at regular intervals of time. The law which I have applied will not only give these long cycles or swings, but the daily and even hourly movements of stocks. By knowing the exact vibration of each individual stock I am able to determine at what point each will receive support and at what point the greatest resistance

18

is to be met.

"Those in close touch with the market have noticed the phenomena of ebb and flow, or rise and fall, in the value of stocks. At certain times a stock will become intensely active, large transactions being made in it; at other times this same stock will become practically stationary or inactive with a very small volume of sales. I have found that the law of vibration governs and controls these conditions. I have also found that certain phases of this law govern the rise in a stock and an entirely different rule operates on the decline."

19

"While Union Pacific and other railroad stocks which made their high prices in August were declining, United States Steel Common was steadily advancing. The law of vibration was at work, sending a particular stock on the upward trend whilst others were trending downward."

"I have found that in the stock itself exists its harmonic or inharmonious relationship to the driving power or force behind it. The secret of all its activity is therefore apparent. By my method I can determine the vibration of each stock and also, by taking certain time values into consideration, I can, in the majority of cases, tell exactly what the stock will do under given conditions."

"The power to determine the trend of the market is due to my knowledge of the characteristics of each individual stock and a certain grouping of different stocks under their proper rates of vibration.

Stocks are like electrons, atoms and molecules, which hold persistently to their own individuality in response to the fundamental law of vibration. Science teaches that an original impulse of any kind finally resolves itself into a periodic or rhythmical motion; also, just as the pendulum returns again in its swing, just

21

as the moon returns in its orbit, just as the advancing year over brings the rose of spring, so do the properties of the elements periodically recur as the weight of the atoms rises."

"From my extensive investigations, studies and applied tests, I find that not only do the various stocks vibrate, but that the driving forces controlling the stocks are also in a state of vibration.

These vibratory forces can only be known by the movements they generate on the stocks and their values in the market. Since all great swings or movements of the market are cyclic, they act in accordance with periodic law."

"Science has laid down the principle that the properties of an element are a periodic function of its atomic weight. A famous scientist has stated that 'we are brought to the conviction that diversity in phenomenal nature in its different kingdoms is most intimately associated with numerical relationship. The numbers are not intermixed accidentally but are subject to regular periodicity. The changes and developments are known to be in many cases as somewhat odd."

Thus, I affirm every class of phenomena, whether in nature or on the stock market, must be subject to the universal law of causation and harmony. Every effect must have an adequate cause.

"If we wish to avert failure in speculation we must deal with causes. Everything in existence is based on exact proportion and perfect relationship. There is no chance in nature, because mathematical principles of the highest order lie at the foundation of all things. Faraday said, "There is nothing in the universe but mathematical points of force."

24

"Vibration is fundamental: nothing is exempt from this law. It is universal, therefore applicable to every class of phenomena on the globe."

Through the law of vibration every stock in the market moves in its own distinctive sphere of activities, as to intensity, volume and direction; all the essential qualities of its evolution are characterized in its own rate of vibration.

Stocks, like atoms, are really centers of energy; therefore, they are controlled mathematically. Stocks create their own field of action and power: power to attract and repel, which principle explains why certain stocks at times lead the market and 'turn dead' at other times. Thus, to speculate scientifically it is absolutely necessary to follow natural law.

"After years of patient study I have proven to my entire satisfaction, as well as demonstrated to others, that vibration explains every possible phase and condition of the market."

***

W.D. GANN INTERVIEW BY RICHARD D. WYCKOFF

W.D. GANN INTERVIEW BY RICHARD D. WYCKOFF

In order to substantiate Mr. W. D. Gann's claims as to what he has been able to do under his method, we called upon Mr. William E. Gilley, an Inspector of Imports, at 16 Beaver Street, New York. Mr. Gilley is well known in the downtown district. He himself has studied stock market movements for twenty-five years, during which time he has examined every piece of market literature that has been issued & procurable in Wall Street. It was he who encouraged Mr. Gann to study the scientific and mathematical possibilities of the subject. When asked what had been the most impressive of Mr. Gann's work and predictions, he replied as follows:

"It is very difficult for me to remember all the predictions and operations of W. D. Gann which may be classed as phenomenal, but the following are a few.

In 1908 when the Union Pacific was 168-1/8, he told me it would not touch 169 before it had a good break. We sold it short all the way down to 152-5/8, covering on the weak spots and putting it out again on the rallies, securing twenty-three points profit out of an eighteen-point market wave."

"He came to me when United States Steel was selling around 50, and said: "This steel will run up to 58 but it will not sell at 59. From there it should break 16 points." We sold it short around 58 with a stop at 59. The highest it went was 58. From there it declined to 41-17 points."

"At another time, wheat was selling at about 89¢. Gann predicted that the May option would sell at $1.35. We bought it and made large profits on the way up. It actually touched $1.35."

"When Union Pacific was 172, he said it would go to 184-7/8 but not an eighth

31

higher until it had a good break. It went to 184-7/8 and came back from there eight or nine times. We sold it short repeatedly, with a stop at 185, and were never caught. It eventually came back to 17."

"Mr. Gann's calculations are based on natural law. I have followed Gann and his work closely for years. I know that he has a firm grasp of the basic principles which govern stock market movements, and I do not believe any other man can duplicate the idea or his method at the present time."

"Early this year, he figured that the top of the advance would fall on a certain day in August and calculated the prices at which the Dow Jones Averages would then stand. The market culminated on the exact day and within four-tenths of one percent of the figures predicted."

"You and W. D. Gann must have cleaned up considerable money on all these operations," was suggested.

"Yes, we have made a great deal of money. Gann has taken half-million dollars out of the market in the past few years. I once saw him take $130, and in less than one month run it up to over

33

$12,000. Gann can compound money faster than any man I have ever met."

"One of the most astonishing calculations made by Mr. Gann was during last summer [1909] when he predicted that September Wheat would sell at $1.20. This meant that it must touch that figure before the end of the month of September. At twelve o'clock, Chicago time, on September 30th (the last day) the option was selling below $1.08, and it looked as though his prediction would not be fulfilled. Mr. Gann said, 'If it does not touch $1.20 by the close of the market it will prove that there is something wrong with my whole

34

method of calculation. I do not care what the price is now, it must go there.' It is common history that September Wheat surprised the whole country by selling at $1.20 and no higher in the very last hour of trading, closing at that figure."

So much for what W. D. Gann has said and done as evidenced by himself & others. Now as to what demonstrations have taken place before our representative:

During the month of October, 1909, in twenty-five market days, W. D. Gann made, in the presence of our representative, two hundred and eighty-

35

six transactions in various stocks, on both the long and short side of the market. Two hundred and sixty-four of these transactions resulted in profits; twenty-two in losses.

The capital with which he operated was doubled ten times, so that at the end of the month he had one thousand percent of his original margin.

In our presence Mr. William D. Gann sold Steel common short at 94-7/8, saying that it would not go to 95. It did not.

On a drive which occurred during the week ending October 29, Mr. Gann bought U.S. Steel common stock at 86-1/4, saying that it would not go to 86. The lowest it sold was 86-1/3.

We have seen Gann give in one day sixteen successive orders in the same stock, eight of which turned out to be at either the top or the bottom eighth of that particular swing. The above we can positively verify.

Such performances as these, coupled with the foregoing, are probably unparalleled in the history of the Street.

37

James R. Koene has said, "The man who is right six times out of ten will make a fortune." Gann is a trader who, without any attempt to make a showing, for he did not know the results were to be published, established a record of over ninety-two percent profitable trades.

Mr. W. D. Gann has refused to disclose his method at any price, but to those scientifically inclined he has unquestionably added to the stock of Wall Street knowledge and pointed out infinite possibilities.

We have requested Mr. Gann to figure out for the readers of the Ticker a few of the most striking indications which appear in his calculations. In presenting these we wish it understood that no man, in or out of Wall Street, is infallible.

William D. Gann's figures, at present, indicate that the trend of the stock market should, barring the usual rallies, be toward the lower prices until March or April 1910.

He calculates that May Wheat, which is now selling at $1.02, should not sell below 99¢, and should sell at $1.45 next spring.

On Cotton, which is now at about 15¢ level, he estimates that after a good reaction from these prices the commodity should reach 18¢ in the spring of 1910. He looks for a corner in the March or May option.

Whether these figures prove correct or not will in no way detract from the record which W. D. Gann has already established.

William Delbert Gann was born in Lufkin, Texas, and is thirty-one years of age. He is a gifted mathematician, has an extraordinary memory for figures, and is an expert Tape Reader. Take away his science and he would beat the market on his intuitive tape reading alone.

Endowed as he is with such qualities, we have no hesitation in predicting that within a comparatively few years, William D. Gann will receive recognition as one of Wall Street's leading operators.

Recommended Readings

- ## Options Made Easy: How to Make Profits Trading in Puts and Calls
  ### By W. D. Gann

To make a success trading in stocks every man should learn everything he can about the stock market and the ways to operate in the market in order to make the greatest success. He should learn to take the smallest risk possible and then try to make the greatest profits possible. The more a man studies and learns the greater success he will have. We quote Proverbs 1: 5- "The wise man will Increase learning." Again, Proverbs 2: 11- "Discretion shall preserve these; understanding shall keep thee. "Proverbs 3: 9- "Give instructions to a wise man and he will become wiser. Teach a just man and he will increase in learning." The "Book of the Lambs" says that the fear of the market is the beginning of knowledge.

- ## 45 Years in Wall Street
  ### By W. D. Gann

In this book I have revealed some of my most valuable rules and secret discoveries never published before, in hopes that others will work and study hard to learn and apply these rules. If they do, speculation and investing will no longer be gambling but will become a

PROFITABLE PROFESSION.

W. D. Gann

- ### The Secret of Gold: How to Get What You Want
  ### By Robert Collier

In this book I shall show you where to find the directions which tell you how to harness this truly illimitable power, how to make it bring to you anything of good you may desire.

- ### The Essence of Success
  ### By Earl Nightingale

- **Invest like a Billionaire: If you are not watching the best investor in the world, who are you watching? (2009)**

Want to check out the best investment management companies?

We pick the cream-of-the-crop portfolio managers and give you access to ALL their holdings.

The following are the investment management companies and their holdings* (for 2008) that you will find in this book:

Warren Buffett - Berkshire Hathaway
George Soros - Fund Management
Richard Aster - Aster Management
Dr. Sam Stewart - Wasatch Advisors
Jim W. Oberweis - Oberweis Management
Arnie Schneider III - Schneider Capital
Scott Satterwhite - Artisan Funds
James Miles - Hotchkis and Wiley
John Keeley - Keeley Asset Management
William B. Frels - Mairs & Power Funds

If you're not following the top investors in the world, who are you following?

9 781638 232636